THE LITTLE RED BOOK OF
FOOTBALL WISDOM

THE LITTLE RED BOOK OF
FOOTBALL WISDOM

Edited by

NIELS AABOE

Skyhorse Publishing

Skyhorse Publishing books may be purchased in bulk
at special discounts for sales promotion, corporate gifts,
fund-raising, or educational purposes. Special editions
can also be created to specifications. For details, contact
the Special Sales Department, Skyhorse Publishing,
307 West 36th Street, 11th Floor, New York,
NY 10018 or info@skyhorsepublishing.com.

Skyhorse® and Skyhorse Publishing® are registered trademarks
of Skyhorse Publishing, Inc.®, a Delaware corporation.

Visit our website at www.skyhorsepublishing.com.

10 9 8 7 6 5 4 3 2 1

Library of Congress Cataloging-in-Publication
Data is available on file.

ISBN: 978-1-62636-080-8

Printed in China

To Alex and Donald
Thanks for going long all those times on Marlborough Road

CONTENTS

INTRODUCTION

In the early 1970s, the comedian George Carlin began performing one of his most famous routines: a hilarious and smart skit on the differences between baseball and American football. Alternately taking on the personas of an addled flower child and cigar-chomping general, Carlin compared the loose poetry of baseball to the military-style structure of football. The bit is very funny, but watching it today, one detects unease beneath the humor. You definitely get the sense that Carlin—who grew up rooting for the Brooklyn Dodgers and later switched to the Mets—knew what was coming: baseball would soon lose its place as America's premier game.

One look at the television ratings for the 2013 Super Bowl will convince even the most die-hard baseball fan that Carlin's premonition has come to pass. Nielsen estimated that of all the TV sets that were switched on while the Baltimore Ravens were battling the San Francisco 49ers, more than 70 percent of them were tuned to the game. Super Bowl XLVII was the third most-watched television event in U.S. history, attracting more than 111 million viewers. Professional football—a game that was once played on sandlots and frozen fields by men who earned most of their money doing other things—is now a global phenomenon.

Since football didn't reach the sports pinnacle overnight, the game has a rich, colorful history, which I've mined for the material included in this book. Careful readers will detect a slight weighting of quotes from the sixties, seventies, and early eighties. The reason for this is that pro football entered the modern television era during this period, which is largely due to talented and innovative players, coaches, owners, and executives like Pete Rozelle, Jim Brown, Lamar Hunt, Joe Namath, Al Davis, and Art Rooney. Along with many others whose words appear in this book, these were groundbreaking figures and personalities whose influence extended well beyond the gridiron.

As pro football grew in popularity, it generated some of the best sports writing of the post-war era. George Plimpton may have started the ball rolling—at least in terms of long-form writing—with *Paper Lion*, published in 1966. In it, Plimpton chronicles a preseason he spent practicing and playing with the Detroit Lions. Along the way, he profiles quite a few of his "teammates" and coaches, many of whom prove to be unexpectedly thoughtful, articulate, and funny.

Jerry Kramer's *Instant Replay*, written with Dick Schaap and published in 1968, takes another tack. The book is a season-long diary, written from a veteran player's perspective. Kramer's description of playing guard for Green Bay Packers' coach Vince Lombardi—whom Kramer and other players alternately revered and hated—is widely considered a sports classic.

In the same category is Roy Blount Jr.'s *About Three Bricks Shy of a Load*, written after the author spent a season with the Pittsburgh Steelers. First published in 1974, Blount's book is an affectionate, hilarious, and sometimes bawdy portrait of a team that stood poised to dominate the NFL for the rest of the decade.

But great football writing and reporting didn't end in the seventies. And players, coaches, broadcasters, and others have never stopped saying memorable things about the game. Vince Lombardi and Knute Rockne are quoted in the collection, of course. But so is Alex Karras, who offers advice on the best way to stop All-Pro running back Jim Brown: "Give each guy on the line an ax." Then there's Randy Cross, offering his opinion of his fellow players' intelligence: "The NFL, like life, is full of idiots." The book includes this glimpse into Bill Parcells's game plan: "If my quarterback runs, I'll shoot him." And no collection of football quotes would be complete without something from "Dandy" Don Meredith, who co-broadcast *Monday Night Football* for eleven years, including this call from a Denver Broncos game: "We're in Mile High Stadium, and I *really* am!"

As these examples suggest, *The Little Red Book of Football Wisdom* offers dozens of wise, witty, and hilariously irreverent quotes about America's most popular sport. Players, coaches, celebrities, politicians, and literary giants weigh in on the best— and worst—football teams, athletes, games, fans, and more.

By the way, it's worth noting that George Carlin eventually became a fan of pro football. Not surprisingly, his favorite team was the Oakland Raiders, a franchise known as much for its outlaw mystique as for occasional on-field success. Carlin expressed his devotion to the team in typically Carlin-esque fashion. He didn't use *all* of the "seven dirty words you can't say on television" (another one of his classic routines), but he came awfully close.

—Niels Aaboe
New York City

Sammy Baugh

PART ONE

THE GAME

Ground acquisition. *That's* what football is, football's a ground acquisition game. You knock the crap out of eleven guys and take their *land* away from them.
—George Carlin

• • •

[F]ootball, truly, is about land. The Settlers want to move the line of scrimmage Westward, the Native Americans want to move it East.
—David Mamet

• • •

[My] obsession with field position—with territory—is a legacy of my coaching days at West Point, where we'd get free advice from every major on campus.
—Bill Parcells

• • •

People get hurt all the time in the game of football, it's part of what we do.
—LAWRENCE TAYLOR

• • •

Football is the expression of the strength of a dominant race, and to this it owes its popularity and its hopes of permanence.
—W. CAMERON FORBES, GRANDSON OF RALPH WALDO EMERSON

• • •

I went to a football school, which meant that I went to a university that served up education and was simultaneously operating a sports franchise.
—SUSAN ORLEAN

• • •

Everyone in my high school was a bit nerdy. We didn't even have a football team.
—NORAH JONES

• • •

After all, is football a game or a religion?
—HOWARD COSELL

• • •

One of my beliefs is that there are certain institutions within a community which stand for the spirit and heart of that community, there's the church, the local football team, the local pub and the theatre.
—David Soul

• • •

It is not simply the violence that spectators . . . celebrate in football, but the human capacity to withstand violence and create something beautiful despite it, or even from it.
—Michael Oriard, from *Reading Football*

• • •

Football players are a simple folk. Whatever complexities, whatever dark politics of the human mind, the heart—these are noted only within the chalked borders of the playing field. At times strange visions ripple across that turf; madness leaks out.
—DON DELILLO, FROM *END ZONE*

• • •

Conventional wisdom notwithstanding, there is no reason either in football or in poetry why the two should not meet in a man's life if he has the weight and cares about the words.
—ARCHIBALD MACLEISH

• • •

Adrian Peterson

In football you have the advantage of players playing different roles from week to week—playing different characters, you might say. In every game they're in different scenes. And that's the reason people will never get tired of this game.
—GEORGE S. HALAS

• • •

There were only two of us in back [of the car]: just me and Richard Nixon, and we were talking football in a very serious way. . . . It was a very weird trip; probably one of the weirdest things I've ever done, and especially weird because both Nixon and I enjoyed it.
—HUNTER S. THOMPSON, FROM *FEAR AND LOATHING ON THE CAMPAIGN TRAIL '72*

• • •

It is veneer, rouge, aestheticism, art museums, new theaters, etc., that make America impotent. The good things are football, kindness, and jazz bands.

—George Santayana

• • •

Academe, n.: An ancient school where morality and philosophy were taught. *Academy*, n.: A modern school where football is taught.

—Ambrose Bierce

• • •

If I was going to get beat up, I wanted it to be indoors where it was warm.

—Former NBA player and coach Tom Heinsohn, on why he chose basketball over football

• • •

I started out as a football player. I liked to inflict pain. In basketball, it was the same thing.
—SHAQUILLE O'NEAL

• • •

Football is an incredible game. Sometimes it's so incredible, it's unbelievable.
—TOM LANDRY

• • •

I mean the game is just, everybody talks about baseball but I really think football probably has a little bit more American feeling than anything.
—JOE MONTANA

• • •

In life, as in a football game, the principle to follow is: Hit the line hard; don't foul and don't shirk, but hit the line hard.
—THEODORE ROOSEVELT

• • •

Politics is like football; if you see daylight, go through the hole.
—JOHN F. KENNEDY

• • •

If I had gone into professional football the name Jerry Ford might have been a household word today.
—GERALD R. FORD

• • •

My dream was to play football for the Oakland Raiders. But my mother thought I would get hurt playing football, so she chose baseball for me. I guess moms do know best.
—Rickey Henderson

• • •

At the base of it was the urge, if you wanted to play football, to knock someone down, that was what the sport was all about, the will to win closely linked with contact.
—George Plimpton

• • •

I don't understand American football at all. It looks like all-in wrestling with crash helmets.
—Sting

• • •

It's weird . . . people say they're not like apes. How do you explain
football then?
—Mitch Hedberg

• • •

Going to college offered me the chance to play football for four
more years.
—Ronald Reagan

• • •

To me the hardest part of being a professional football player is
on the one hand you're a millionaire and on the other they blow a
whistle and you have to run around after a football.
—Jerry Seinfeld

• • •

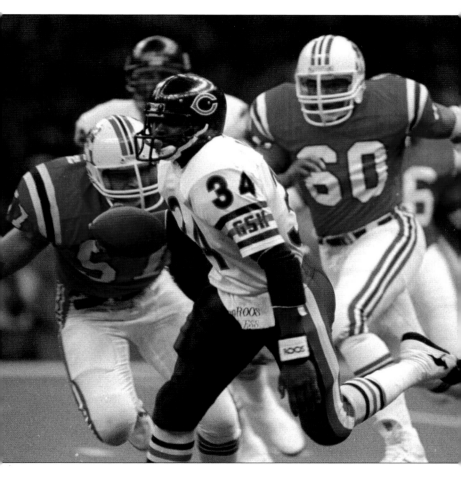

Walter Payton

Pro football gave me a good sense of perspective to enter politics: I'd already been booed, cheered, cut, sold, traded and hung in effigy.
—Former NFL QB and U.S. Senator Jack Kemp

• • •

There are several differences between a football game and a revolution. For one thing, a football game usually lasts longer and the participants wear uniforms.
—Alfred Hitchcock

• • •

I'm not particularly interested in scrambling and creating, because that's where you create interceptions, that's where you create problems. We don't want jazz musicians. We want classical musicians.
—Pittsburgh Steelers coach Chuck Noll

• • •

I love football. I really love football. As far as I'm concerned, it's the second-best thing in the world.
—JOE NAMATH

• • •

I like sex as much as Joe Namath does. I just have it with one woman.
—ROGER STAUBACH

• • •

I can't believe these salaries [today]. All we needed in the old days was enough dough to buy a hunk of kosher salami, a loaf of Jewish rye, and a case of Schlitz.
—ART DONOVAN, WHO PLAYED IN THE NFL FROM 1950 TO 1961

• • •

I feel like football players are overworked and underpaid compared to any other sports.
—TERRELL OWENS

• • •

When I played, not one guy on the team weighed 300 pounds. Now you've got guys coming in at 350 and 360 pounds. They're just trying to suck in air now. It would be impossible for them to play two ways. They are a bunch of overweight, fat pigs.
—HALL OF FAME TWO-WAY PLAYER CHUCK BEDNARIK (PHILADELPHIA EAGLES, 1949–1962)

• • •

Ours was the great era of professional football, because it was the players game then. It's the coaches' game now. In those days quarterbacks looked their own guys right in the eye, and then stared across the line at the other guys. Who's ready to do it? Who's starting to quit? We controlled the game.
—SONNY JURGENSEN, NFL QB FROM 1957 TO 1974

• • •

It doesn't matter how good you are and what your loyalty is to a team. Professional football is a business and you will get replaced. It was a business back when I broke in and it has grown tenfold since.

—JERRY RICE

• • •

Football nowadays is on a much different scale. . . . It's big-money business. It's important, and there isn't anything very funny in it. I think in the old days we had more laughs and more unusual experiences to remember, because when a fellow's making seventy-five or a hundred dollars a game, he can have a few laughs. The fate of the nation did not depend on whether you won or lost.

—RED GRANGE

• • •

Because football once existed before replay—and before television, for that matter—we still must deal with the grumpy-old-men argument that we shouldn't remove the human element from the game. All that means is that we know the officials will make mistakes, but let's not do anything to correct the errors. Nonsense.
—PAUL ATTNER

• • •

There's a blissfully simple explanation why replay should be beanbagged: It's not fun. You know what's fun? Hut-hut-hike, violent tackle. Replay keeps us from that.
—STEVE GREENBERG

• • •

I always figured being a little dull was part of being a pro. I never walked off the football field without thinking of something boring to say to [the press].
—Johnny Unitas

• • •

He broke his nose really badly, they literally called a timeout and then they called another one while they stopped the bleeding, they stuck stuff up there until it would stop bleeding. You try to get them to do that today. They would be yelling, "Get my agent!"
—Frank Gifford, on his Giants teammate Charlie Conerly

• • •

Life was simpler when me and Shake Tiller and D.J. played. The quarterback didn't wear an evening gown and a string of pearls. Pass interference was when you broke a guy's ribs. Today it's excessive frowning.
—Dan Jenkins, from *Rude Behavior* (1999)

• • •

We take most of our players out of Southern colleges and are trying to appeal to Southern people. Those colleges don't have any Negro players.
—George Preston Marshall, owner of the Washington Redskins, in a *New York Times* interview in 1961

• • •

In modern pro football, Marshall is an anachronism, as out of date as the drop-kick. The other club owners have passed him by. Marshall, with his dedication to white supremacy on the football field, is still hearing a cry that doesn't exist.
—Shirley Povich

• • •

Look at a football field. It looks like a big movie screen. This is theatre. Football combines the strategy of chess. It's part ballet. It's part battleground, part playground.
—Steve Sabol

• • •

Football was Mr. Kennedy's game.
—COMMISSIONER PETE ROZELLE, ON HIS DECISION TO PLAY
A COMPLETE SCHEDULE OF NFL GAMES TWO DAYS AFTER
THE ASSASSINATION OF PRESIDENT KENNEDY

• • •

In the afternoon, I went to the Giants' game. We had a moment of silence. I could not concentrate on the game. I brooded about my decision the entire game. You have to understand, I was more than depressed over the assassination. I had lost someone whom I'd respected as the leader of our country, but I was also a close friend of the Kennedy family.
—PETE ROZELLE, REFLECTING ON HIS DECISION YEARS LATER

• • •

We wanted to be sensitive, certain, and right, and certainly not superficial. At a certain point playing our games can contribute to the healing process. Just not at this time.
—COMMISSIONER PAUL TAGLIABUE, ON HIS DECISION TO
CANCEL NFL GAMES AFTER THE TERRORIST ATTACKS OF
SEPTEMBER 11, 2001

• • •

I wouldn't ever set out to hurt somebody unless it was important,
like a league game or something.
—ALL-PRO LINEBACKER DICK BUTKUS

• • •

I am not a dirty player. I have at certain times had violent urges,
but I don't think I ever have hurt anybody. Tried to a couple of
times, but I don't think I have. Yeah, guess I have.
—"MEAN" JOE GREENE

• • •

To me, football is a contest in embarrassments. The quarterback is out there to embarrass me in front of my friends, my teammates, my coach, my wife, and my three boys. The quarterback doesn't leave me any choice: I've got to embarrass him instead.
—ALL-PRO DEFENSIVE LINEMAN ALEX KARRAS

• • •

I had sacrificed my entire life to play football.
—BRIAN BOSWORTH

• • •

Baseball players are smarter than football players. How often do you see baseball players punished for having too many men on the field?
—JIM BOUTON

• • •

Football features two of the worst aspects of American life—
violence and committee meetings.
—GEORGE WILL

• • •

You could run faster if you didn't have that thing on your lip.
—VINCE LOMBARDI TO A REDSKIN ROOKIE, WHO THEN
SHAVED HIS MUSTACHE AT LUNCHTIME

• • •

Football is a wonderful way to get rid of aggressiveness without
going to jail for it.
—HEYWOOD HALE BROUN

• • •

Pro football is like nuclear warfare. There are no winners—
only survivors.
—Frank Gifford

• • •

I have to tell you if I had a son, I'd have to think long and hard
before I let him play football.
—President Barack Obama

• • •

If my mother put on a helmet and shoulder pads and a uniform
that wasn't the same as the one I was wearing, I'd run over her if
she was in my way. And I love my mother.
—Bo Jackson

• • •

Only angry people win football games.
—Darryl Royal

• • •

I don't feel pain from a hit like that. What I feel is joy. Joy for the tackle. Joy for myself. Joy for the other man. You understand me; I understand you. It's football.
—Chicago Bears linebacker Mike Singletary

• • •

I sent Gifford some fruit in the hospital. And I wrote him a three-page letter. It was a good tackle.
—Chuck Benarik, reflecting on his devastating hit on the Giants' Frank Gifford

• • •

I wasn't necessarily drawn to [football] itself; I simply loved what came with the sport: respect.
—Howie Long

• • •

Football is a game played with arms and legs and shoulders, but
mainly from the neck up.
—KNUTE ROCKNE

• • •

Football is blocking and tackling. Everything else is mythology.
—VINCE LOMBARDI

• • •

Blocking, unlike running a 4.5 forty, can be mastered by anyone
who is exposed to a good teacher.
—FROM *COACHING OFFENSIVE LINEMEN*

• • •

I enjoy springing a back loose, making a good trap block, a good solid trap block, cutting down my man the way I'm supposed to. But I'm not quite as boyish about the whole thing as I used to be.
—JERRY KRAMER, FROM *INSTANT REPLAY*

• • •

When I was playing lacrosse in high school, I couldn't wait for practice because I got to play lacrosse. Football practice isn't like that.
—BILL BELICHICK

• • •

A few plays decide each football game.
—VINCE LOMBARDI

• • •

Every team . . . has players good enough to make you lose. They're fast, they're strong, they look good in the uniform, they say all the right things, but they don't deliver. It's the guy who misses his block on fourth-and-one, it's the back who fumbles . . . . They're great in practice, but in the game they're just good enough to make you lose.
—George Allen

• • •

Football isn't a contact sport—it's a collision sport. Dancing is a contact sport.
—Former college coach Duffy Daugherty

• • •

If you play one regular season game in the National Football League, you will never, ever be normal physically.
—John Madden

• • •

We try to hurt each other. We try to hurt each other as hard as we can. This is a man's game.
—ALL-PRO LINEBACKER SAM HUFF

• • •

I just thought it was a knock against you if you didn't play—unless you couldn't walk. If I wasn't on a stretcher, I could play—that's the way I looked at it.
—JOE KLECKO, NEW YORK JETS

• • •

Put a bull and a cat in an arena and have them run at each other. What do you think the bull is thinking? When I cover somebody, that's what I'm thinking.
—CHARLES WOODSON, GREEN BAY PACKERS DEFENSIVE BACK

• • •

If you want to surf, move to Hawaii. If you like to shop, move to New York. If you like acting and Hollywood, move to California. But if you like college football, move to Texas.
—RICKY WILLIAMS

• • •

I can't remember how many times I got hit so hard I lost my memory.
—TERRY BRADSHAW

• • •

Before you can win the game you have to not lose it.
—CHUCK NOLL

• • •

At some point, football just comes down to willpower.
—BRIAN SHOTTENHEIMER

• • •

The kickoff team is football's greatest test of courage. It's the way
we find out who likes to hit.
—VINCE LOMBARDI

• • •

If you want to play long in the NFL . . . don't return kickoffs.
—JERRY TUBBS, FORMER ASSISTANT COACH FOR THE
DALLAS COWBOYS

• • •

Everything in life has a price on it—there ain't a damn thing free
in America, and football has got a price on it.
—EARL CAMPBELL

• • •

Fortunately, in my position you don't have to learn plays or new
formations. It's just catch it and kick it. That's pretty universal
throughout the league. . . . So I'll just keep doing what I've been
doing for fifteen years. It's just a different venue, different city.
—CHRIS MOHR, WHO PUNTED FOR THE TAMPA BAY
BUCCANEERS, BUFFALO BILLS, AND ATLANTA FALCONS

• • •

Football is all work. You wouldn 't play football if you could do something else and make money. Because every time you get on the field you put your health in danger.
—Pittsburgh Steeler Mel Blount

• • •

We prided ourselves on hitting harder than anybody, even after the whistle. We bent the rules we didn't break.
—Oakland Raiders center Jim Otto

• • •

Our first-round draft pick caught a pass, and I hit him hard and knocked him out. The coach said, "Great play." So I knew what I had to do to make the team. The vets got so mad at me because I really hit. They would say that it's just training camp. But it wasn't training camp for me. I was fighting for a job.
—FORMER EAGLE TOM BROOKSHIER

• • •

Veterans don't love rookies. It's as simple as that. . . . A regular, particularly an old-timer, will do almost anything to hold onto his position short of murder.
—JOE SCHMIDT, DETROIT LIONS LINEBACKER

• • •

You don't remember the [games] you win 35-17. You remember the ones you win 38-35. A two-minute drive. They score. You score. Those are the ones that are memorable. Who wants everything to come easy?
—NEW ENGLAND PATRIOTS QB TOM BRADY

• • •

Basically, every football team has a pattern. It is the purpose of scouting, and the analysis of scouting, to establish what the pattern is and how to defend as best you can against the strength and take advantage of the weaknesses.
—STEVE BELICHICK, FROM *FOOTBALL SCOUTING METHODS*

• • •

Football, like baseball, is all about forecasting. Coaches build their entire game plans around tendencies—what their opponent's track record suggests they might do in certain situations.
—PAT KIRWAN, FROM *TAKE YOUR EYE OFF THE BALL*

• • •

In the 1960s, a squeaky voiced [Don Coryell of the San Diego Chargers] decided there was only one way to beat a better team: Throw like hell.
—TOM LAYDEN, FROM *BLOOD, SWEAT, AND CHALK: HOW THE GREAT COACHES BUILT TODAY'S GAME*

• • •

Lombardi's power sweep: Here was one man's proof that a key to football will always be knocking the crap out of somebody else at the line of scrimmage.
—TOM LAYDEN, FROM *BLOOD, SWEAT, AND CHALK: HOW THE GREAT COACHES BUILT TODAY'S GAME*

• • •

The quarterback position is the cornerstone of any modern offense. Unfortunately, there are not enough naturally gifted athletes around to play the position effectively enough to win on a consistent basis.
—RON JENKINS, FROM *QUARTERBACK PLAY: FUNDAMENTALS AND TECHNIQUES*

• • •

If Tiger Woods had played football, he would have been a quarterback.
—LOU HOLTZ

• • •

Sure, luck means a lot in football. Not having a good quarterback
is bad luck.
—DON SHULA

• • •

My philosophy is that you've got to hit the quarterback.
—HERMAN EDWARDS

• • •

For a kid who's lost his mom and all the rage and grief that no one was able to talk out of me, football was a very therapeutic sport. Very.
—John Hamm

• • •

I want to play until I'm 41. And if I get to that point and still feel good, I'll keep playing. I mean, what the hell else am I going to do? I don't like anything else.
—Tom Brady

• • •

I love the game so much. I've been penalized. I've been fined.
I have some regrets in my career. But for those four hours on
Sunday, you can be free and just let it all go.
—RANDY MOSS

• • •

The saddest day of my life was the day I didn't get to play
football anymore.
—BRIAN BOSWORTH

• • •

Barry Sanders

PART TWO

THE PLAYERS

You can lose with good football players, but you can never, ever win without them.
—ART ROONEY JR.

• • •

If they're sloppy, or drinkers, or chasers, or whiners, it will show up eventually.
—CLEVELAND BROWNS COACH PAUL BROWN

• • •

[QB Bobby Layne] never lost a game, really—time just ran out on him. That's not a bad man to have around as a leader.
—DETROIT LION BOB SCHOTZ

• • •

It's like being in the huddle with God.
—BALTIMORE COLTS TIGHT END JOHN MACKEY, ON PLAYING WITH JOHNNY UNITAS

• • •

You couldn't shake [Unitas]. Once in a while the defense got in there, knocked him down, stomped on him, and hurt him. The test of a great quarterback is what he did next. Unitas would get up, call another play, and drop back into the pocket. Out of the corner of his eye he might see you coming again. . .then he threw it on the button.
—LA RAMS DEFENSIVE END MERLIN OLSEN

• • •

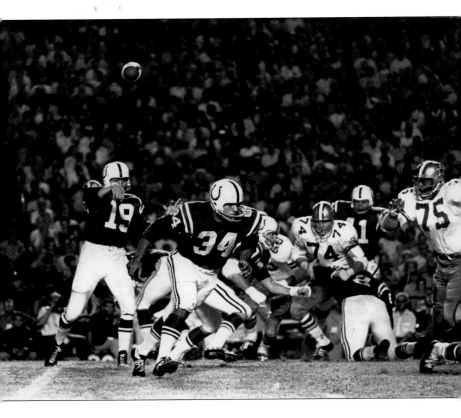

Johnny Unitas

Quarterbacks were [once] field generals, not field lieutenants.
I never saw war, so that is still my vision of manhood: Unitas
standing courageously in the pocket, down amidst the mortals.
Lock and load.
—Frank Deford

• • •

Football is such a great game, but football players are so dull.
—Steve Sabol

• • •

We had the fifth pick in the [1957] draft, and we liked Lenny
[Dawson] more than John Brodie. . .We had to content ourselves
with a running back from Syracuse named Jim Brown.
—Dick Gallagher, personnel chief of the
Cleveland Browns

• • •

I hit that big sucker [Jim Brown] head on. He broke my nose,
broke my teeth, knocked me cold.
—NY Giants linebacker Sam Huff

• • •

Anybody that's ever played with Jim Brown or against him will
tell you that he's by far the best running back ever.
—Cleveland linebacker Vince Costello

• • •

[Jim Brown] gets off to the quickest start of any big man I've ever
seen. An arm tackle is no soap; he runs right though you. The
only way I've found to stop him is to hit him right at the ankles
with your shoulder. . . . Otherwise, it's like tackling a locomotive.
—Glenn Holzman of the Los Angeles Rams

• • •

Jim Brown

We'll miss [Paul] Hornung. The other fellow we'll replace.
—Vince Lombardi, after Paul Hornung retired and
Jim Taylor signed with another team for more money
in the same year

• • •

[Dick Butkus's] name is synonymous with his position and
brutal, old school football.
—Tim Layden, *Sports Illustrated*, on the Chicago
Bears linebacker

• • •

Mr. Jim Brown, someday I'm going to break all your records.
—a young O.J. Simpson

• • •

Being the best is something I've lived with. And I like living with it.
—O.J. Simpson

• • •

O.J. is extremely smart, man knows how to make a buck, and his "aw shucks" image is his meal ticket. He's not about to jeopardize that by being honest.
—Jim Brown

• • •

Playing defense in practice against Gale [Sayers], I knew what the other teams had to go through. I had never met a guy who could stop on a dime and go full speed in the opposite direction. I just couldn't believe this guy. He was absolutely the best.
—Dick Butkus

• • •

Just give me 18 inches of daylight. . . . That's all I need.
—GALE SAYERS

• • •

[Sonny] Werblin told me I was the greatest college football player
he had ever seen, and if I came to the Jets he would give me the
same deal he gave Joe Namath. . . . I ended up in Denver.
—FLOYD LITTLE

• • •

What was it like to play against Deacon Jones? How did people
feel about Attila the Hun?
—BART STARR

• • •

I've never seen anyone hit like [Dick "Night Train" Lane]. I mean, take them down, whether it be Jim Brown or Jim Taylor.
—GREEN BAY PACKER HERB ADDERLEY

• • •

I think about Alex [Karras] all the time, morning, noon, and night, even when I'm watching television. I think about the way he's built, like a bowling ball, and I think about his strength. . . . But most of my thoughts are vicious.
—JERRY KRAMER, FROM *INSTANT REPLAY*

• • •

[Alex Karras] has everything, the Johnny Unitas of his position—instinct, size, ability, the moves of a ballet dancer, dainty . . .
—NICK PIETROSANTE, A TEAMMATE OF KARRAS'S ON THE DETROIT LIONS

• • •

There were runners who made you miss, like O.J. and Floyd
Little, and runners who'd go through you, like [Larry] Csonka
and John Riggins. Franco [Harris] did both.
—ANDY RUSSELL

• • •

When we saw films of the second Houston game last year, we
sat by the phone waiting for the league office to call up and say
they were going to put Joe [Greene] in jail. He just beat on the
poor guy.
—PITTSBURGH STEELERS EXECUTIVE ART ROONEY JR.

• • •

Joe Greene was unquestionably the NFL's best player in the seventies. No player had a greater impact or did more for his team.
—ANDY RUSSELL, FROM A STEELER ODYSSEY

• • •

The Steelers have a number of stars and leaders of various kinds, but Greene is their sun. The main strength of the team is their defense, of the defense the front four, of the front four, Greene.
—ROY BLOUNT JR.

● ● ●

I was having too much trouble destroying your offense to get kicked out of the game—for fighting with that wildman rookie of yours.
—DICK BUTKUS, WHEN ASKED WHY HE BACKED DOWN FROM A FIGHT WITH JOE GREENE

● ● ●

Some guys took low levels of amphetamines before games. They were called crop dusters. Others indulged more heavily. They were 747s. The Tooz was called John Glenn.
—ROB HUIZENGA, FORMER OAKLAND RAIDERS PHYSICIAN, ON DEFENSIVE LINEMAN JOHN MATUSZAK

● ● ●

As an announcer of himself to hotel desk clerks, [Pittsburgh Steeler defensive end Dwight White] was expansive: "That's me. The man who walked the water and tied the wind, come to bring good to your neighborhood. You can see me free till Sunday."
—Roy Blount Jr., from *About Three Bricks Shy of a Load*

• • •

With just a flick of the wrist, he could put it in the end zone from about the 35-yard line. I mean, other guys could take a running start and throw it that far. Joe just did it with such ease. Like he was throwing a baseball.
—A teammate of Joe Namath's at the University of Alabama

• • •

Joe Namath had more natural playing ability than anybody.
—Paul "Bear" Bryant

• • •

If I had good knees, I might have gotten killed in Vietnam.
—Joe Namath

• • •

After a look at Joe Namath in pulsating color, I'm convinced of one thing. The Jets aren't paying him enough.
—New York Daily News columnist Dick Young

• • •

Joe Namath

You're Terry Bradshaw. I've seen Ruth, Man O' War, Dempsey, Ty Cobb. You're right with those guys.
—ART ROONEY TO STEELERS QB TERRY BRADSHAW

• • •

The fact of the matter is that [Roger Staubach] had to work long and hard to become a Heisman Trophy winner, a Super Bowl MVP, and a Hall of Fame inductee. He was never the biggest or strongest or fastest. He reached great heights by being an incredible competitor.
—FORMER DALLAS COWBOYS WIDE RECEIVER
DREW PEARSON

• • •

Roger Staubach was a great NFL quarterback, and certainly in my top three as the best who ever played the game.
—FRAN TARKENTON

• • •

We've got a rookie so mean, he doesn't even like himself.
—Pittsburgh Steelers defensive line coach George Perles, on Jack Lambert in 1974

• • •

Jack Lambert, the middle linebacker, is considered wild, but not mean, not sneaky.
—Dave Anderson, *New York Times*

• • •

Tony Dorsett was fast through the hole and could shift to a gear designed for raw speed that we had never seen before. He was a phenom.
—Dallas Cowboys safety Cliff Harris

• • •

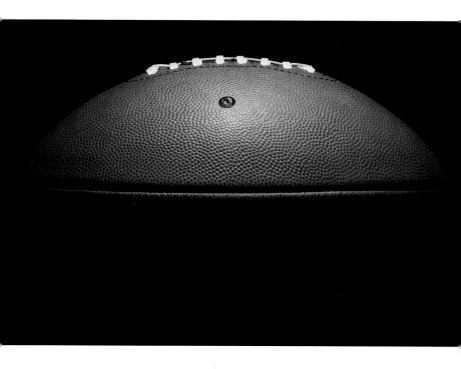

I was so happy [to be drafted by Dallas in 1978]. I wanted to play
for America's team.
—TONY DORSETT

• • •

When [Miami Dolphins running back] Larry Csonka wanted to
gain three yards, there didn't seem to be enough defensive players
to prevent him from doing it. . . . Csonka was the guy who Bills
fans hated the most.
—BUFFALO BILLS GUARD JOE DELAMIELLEURE

• • •

Joe [Montana] could make plays on the move or in the pocket.
He was a master at going through his progression of receivers
and finding the open man.
—SAN FRANCISCO 49ERS RUNNING BACK ROGER CRAIG

• • •

What if Tampa Bay or New Orleans would have taken [Joe Montana]? What if he had been in a system where he had to drop back seven steps and throw 50 yards downfield?
—Joe Montana's high school coach

• • •

There's no coach [other than Bill Walsh] who I could have played for who would have been better for my career. Absolutely none.
—Joe Montana

• • •

It was like this guy [Joe Montana] was touched by God, he's designed to play for the 49ers. He's gonna be indestructible.
—Carmen Policy

• • •

Joe Montana and Bill Walsh

[Steve] Young has the mobility that 49ers coach Bill Walsh prizes in quarterbacks—he even was used as a running back at times by the Los Angeles Express—and he's an accurate passer. He is, in fact, much like Joe Montana when Montana first came to the 49ers.

—GLENN DICKEY, *SAN FRANCISCO CHRONICLE*

• • •

He was just everything you want in a great, big running back. You didn't hit John [Riggins]; John hit you.

—JOE THEISMANN

• • •

The biggest misconception is that [John Riggins] is a clown. He's not a clown; he's a showman instead. He knows intuitively the right thing to do and yet do it in a colorful way.

—JACK KENT COOKE JR.

• • •

John even went to George Allen one time and said, "Hey, why don't you give me a 60 [jersey] number since I'm only going to get the ball once or twice a game?"
—RON SAUL

• • •

I'm thinking about adding another hobby to my off-season curriculum, and that's all that it would be.
—BO JACKSON, PLAYING FOR THE KANSAS CITY ROYALS, ON SIGNING WITH THE OAKLAND RAIDERS

• • •

My workout was running down fly balls, stealing a base, or running for my life on the football field.
—BO JACKSON

• • •

I tossed the ball to Bo, a little sweep to the left side. It looked like Deion Sanders had an angle on him, and then [Bo] just left him. [Deion] was beside him, and then he was behind him.
—Pat Washington

• • •

Once we measured John's thighs, and they were 33 inches. I said, "I can't bear it. They're bigger than my bust."
—Page Hannah, referring to her husband, Patriots guard John Hannah

• • •

Tim Rossovich was the most talented big man I ever knew. He was also the craziest man I ever knew. Absolutely fearless. He was strong and talented, fun and exciting.
—Norm Snead

• • •

[Joe Theismann] played you to the end. Always. Every game, every down. He was the ultimate competitor.
—DALLAS COWBOY RANDY WHITE

• • •

Earl Campbell had some collisions with our players. I think he won them all.
—MIAMI DOLPHINS COACH DON SHULA, AFTER THE ROOKIE OILERS RUNNING BACK RAN FOR 199 YARDS ON *MONDAY NIGHT FOOTBALL*

• • •

[Offensive lineman Antony Munoz] was so big and so good it was a joke.
—MIKE BROWN, ASSISTANT GM OF THE CINCINNATI BENGALS

• • •

Sometimes I wonder if this kid is actually as good as I think he is.
—JACK ELWAY, ON HIS SON, YOUNG JOHN ELWAY

• • •

[John Elway] was the best-looking college football player I've ever seen. He had it all. The arm. The athleticism. The physique. The football mentality. . . . He really was a once-in-a-lifetime football player.
—PAUL WIGGIN, FORMER COACH AT STANFORD AND NFL SCOUT

• • •

"Do I really belong in the National Football League?" I remember thinking, "Do I really belong on the Denver Broncos to be so lucky and fortunate to catch passes from John Elway?"
—SHANNON SHARPE

• • •

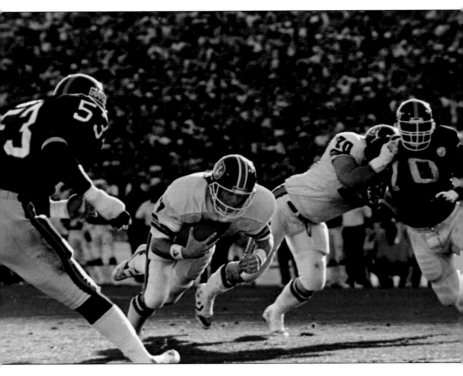

John Elway

Mark Gastineau was one of a kind. . . . Mark was probably pound
for pound, for a man over 280 pounds, the best athlete I've ever
seen. He could run. He was certainly the fastest.
—CHRIS WARD, GASTINEAU'S TEAMMATE ON THE
NEW YORK JETS

● ● ●

Gastineau was one of the best pass-rushing defensive lineman
I've ever seen . . . , but [he] didn't care much about the run.
—DAN ALEXANDER

● ● ●

Look, no matter what happens, you know you can play, and you
know you're as good as any of these guys picked ahead of you.
You'll have your opportunity to prove it.
—DAN MARINO'S FATHER TO HIS SON, ON NFL DRAFT DAY IN
1983, WHEN MARINO WAS CHOSEN 27TH OVERALL

● ● ●

Dan Marino was the best passer in NFL history.
—Don Shula, Marino's coach with
the Miami Dolphins

• • •

The most sincere voice mail I got after the Super Bowl [victory] was from Dan Marino. He did the coin toss that day, and he said it was an honor to be on the field with me. I'll remember that for a long time.
—Peyton Manning

• • •

The most amazing thing to watch is [Bruce Smith's] rush. . . . I can't figure it out—it's like a speedskater coming around a corner, he's so low to the ground, almost flat, with offensive lineman literally chasing him.
—Buffalo Bills center Kent Hull

• • •

Eric will be our No. 1 objective. I've seen enough of Dickerson
to know just how tremendous he can be. He's done as well as
anybody I've ever seen coming into this league
—Tom Landry, before his Cowboys faced Dickerson
for the first time as a pro

• • •

The Rams got me cheap, and everyone knows it. I need to get the
money now while I'm still healthy, while I'm whole. But I'll settle
for a million.
—Eric Dickerson, who set the single-season rushing
record of 2,105 yards in 1984

• • •

There was a time, not so long ago, when teams were simply
scared to play the Giants. They looked at their linebackers, they
saw people like Harry Carson and Lawrence Taylor, and they
stayed up late finding ways to stop them.
—Mike Freeman

• • •

Lawrence Taylor

Buffalo coach Marv Levy to center Will Grant: "You've been called for holding [Lawrence Taylor] six times in one half!" Grant to Levy: "Hey, Coach, that's really good. Because I've been holding him on every down."
—MARV LEVY, FROM *WHERE ELSE WOULD YOU RATHER BE?*

• • •

Great defenses, cold weather, Lawrence Taylor, Bill Parcells. That was Giants football.
—JOHN MADDEN

• • •

I think all of us in the late 80s and early 90s made receiving a critical position in an offense which required speed, height, and an ability to make big plays—and that's the prototypical wide receiver position today.
—JERRY RICE

• • •

Mentally and physically he is the toughest guy I've ever played with in my 11 years. He is probably the most versatile running back in the N.F.L. in the last 9 to 10 years. Ask any linebacker in the N.F.L. what running back they'd hate most to cover and it's Marcus [Allen].
—Howie Long

• • •

I'm paying him $1.1 million. That's what I think of him.
—Oakland Raiders owner Al Davis, when asked what he thinks of running back Marcus Allen

• • •

The good part is, I'm going to have a chance to play pretty quickly. The way they've talked, I can be the man up there.
—Brett Favre, after he was traded from the Atlanta Falcons to the Green Bay Packers

• • •

You are my guy, and we are joined at the hip. We are either going to get to the top of the mountain together or we are going to wind up in the dumpster together. But we are going to be together.
—Mike Holmgren, Brett Favre's first coach in Green Bay

• • •

[Brett Favre's] numbers are getting so wide, they won't fit on the television screen. . . . They're going to need DDTV.
—John Madden

• • •

They put the stadium upgrade to a referendum. Why not vote on whether or not to keep Brett Favre?
—A Green Bay Packers fan, after Favre was released by the team

• • •

I thought about being a professional athlete from the time I was eight years old. I never thought it wouldn't happen.
—DALLAS COWBOYS QB TROY AIKMAN

• • •

Day in and day out Troy Aikman developed into the perfect quarterback. Some players are good in practices and better in games. Troy was the same everywhere—absolutely awesome.
—FORMER DALLAS COWBOYS QB CLIFF STOUDT

• • •

Coach [Bill] Walsh looked me in the eye and said, "Roger we're going to need 1,000 yards from you this season. I was fired up . . . but then I started to wonder if he meant he needed 1,000 yards rushing, or receiving. . . . I wanted to cover my ass, so I figured I'd better get 1,000 yards rushing and receiving.
—ROGER CRAIG, WHO RUSHED FOR 1,050 YARDS AND CAUGHT PASSES FOR 1,016 YARDS IN 1985

• • •

There is nobody like him [Barry Sanders]. There have been maybe two other guys in the history of the game like him that impact a game from that position: Jim Brown and Walter Payton. That's it. . . . If we had him, he'd get the ball 30 to 35 times a game and he would catch it 10 times a game, too.

—Bobby Beathard, GM of the San Diego Chargers

• • •

It doesn't matter where the play is blocked; he'll find his own soft spot. . . . While other people are stuck with joints, he seems to have ball bearings in his legs that give him a mechanical advantage. . . . Sanders' finest runs often occur when he takes the handoff and, with a couple of moves, turns the line of scrimmage into a broken field.

—Paul Zimmerman, Sports Illustrated

• • •

I was worth the money and more. I was MVP of the league and the Super Bowl.

—Dallas Cowboys running back Emmitt Smith, on his season in 1993, which began with a contract dispute

• • •

Emmitt was a football messiah, delivered to Dallas by the gods of the game.
—COWBOYS WIDE RECEIVER DENNIS MCKINNON

• • •

It's not important to be known as someone who hits hard. It's important to be known as someone who gives his all.
—DEFENSIVE BACK RONNIE LOTT

• • •

I felt weak and had hot and cold flashes. I didn't think I could put on a Walter Payton-type performance. . . .[but] the holes were there, and I just ran.
—WALTER PAYTON, AFTER GAINING 274 YARDS ON 40 CARRIES AGAINST THE MINNESOTA VIKINGS ON NOVEMBER 20, 1977

• • •

[Reggie White] was a great guy to coach. Very productive. Golly, he had so many pass-rush techniques. If one didn't work, he would counter with the other one. . . . You couldn't stop him. Offensive lineman, boy, they were shaking in their boots on Sunday morning. What a great job he did.
—Dale Haupt, Philadelphia line coach during White's career with the Eagles

• • •

If Randy Moss had the drive to be great, he could be the greatest wide receiver to play the game—he's that good. His size and speed and ability to get open make him virtually untouchable. But Randy is more of a follower than a leader, and plays up to his abilities only when he wants to. . . .
—Jerry Rice

• • •

If [Randy Moss] went to the bathroom, I went, too.
—Darrelle Revis, Tampa Bay Buccaneers defensive back

• • •

I was never good. I was always great.
—Deion Sanders

• • •

When a guy like Deion is on the other team and going through his antics and showboating, you tend not to like him. When he gets on your team and you see that it's just part of his personality and you get to know the person—not just the player—then you find out what a good person and teammate he is.
—Former Dallas special teams coach Joe Avezzano

• • •

I'll have to be honest. I never liked Deion Sanders. Too much of a showboat for me. Now I'm going to spend eternity with him because he is trusting in Christ.
—Deion Sanders

• • •

[Donovan] McNabb played on broken ankles and got to Pro Bowls and yet in his first five years, what was the biggest story? The Rush Limbaugh controversy in which the then-ESPN analyst called McNabb overrated and said he got great treatment from the media because they were "desirous of a black quarterback to do well." . . . It's too bad—because getting to five conference championship games when you're the only constant from those teams is incredibly impressive.

—JASON SMITH

• • •

[Ray Lewis] chases down ball carriers as if he were a human Pac-Man. Plus, his pregame introductions are enough to make spectators want to go out and hit someone.

—JIM TROTTER, SPORTS ILLUSTRATED

• • •

Ray Lewis

He doesn't let anything bother him. It's very hard for me to understand how he does that.
—NEW YORK GIANT MICHAEL STRAHAN ON QB ELI MANNING

• • •

Walk around New England today, and you'll encounter more than your fair share of longtime Patriot fans who swear they always saw something special in [Tom] Brady. Fans who'll insist they knew Brady was the guy who could lead the Patriots to new heights. They're mostly lying.
—SEAN GLENNON, FROM *TOM BRADY VS. THE NFL*

• • •

I thought Michael [Vick] played great. He can run around a lot better than I can. They would have carted me off if I'd have run that far.
—BRETT FAVRE

• • •

[Running back Ricky Williams] can be such a physical, brutal force, but off the field he's very soft-spoken and such a teddy bear. That's another of his dualities.
—Filmmaker Sean Pamphilon

• • •

Well, I don't think I've necessarily ever been a passionate football player or a passionate person.
—Ricky Williams

• • •

I don't know if I had a daughter if I'd want her to date him, but as a football player, as a teammate, I love him.
—Channing Crowder, Miami Dolphins linebacker, on Ricky Williams

• • •

My dad told me before the draft: You're going to be the No. 1 pick and you're going to a bad team. This is how it works.
—Peyton Manning on being drafted by the Indianapolis Colts in 1998

• • •

Here we are. I'm at my third Pro Bowl. I'm about to throw a touchdown to Jerry Rice, we're honoring the Hall of Fame, and we're talking about our idiot kicker who got liquored up and ran his mouth off.
—Indianapolis Colts QB Peyton Manning, on Colts kicker Mike Vanderjagt

• • •

I never was one to believe in chemistry, but you had to notice that we'd always brought in the same kind of guys, guys who didn't care about the spotlight or about stats, guys that just wanted to win. You bring in one guy who doesn't feed into that thinking and it disrupts the whole team.
—Philadelphia Eagle N. D. Kalu, after the team released Terrell Owens

• • •

It's not only about having great hands and strength but also balance. I have to engage this guy while he's sprinting toward me and I'm moving back. Without balance I'll fall, and he'll be past me.

—BALTIMORE RAVENS OFFENSIVE TACKLE JONATHAN OGDEN

• • •

Losing in the [2010] AFC championship was tough enough, but having Peyton Manning take a second Super Bowl ring from me just pissed me off. . . . You have to win against the best, and Peyton Manning is the best.

—REX RYAN

• • •

[Broncos defensive back] Champ Bailey needs to lighten up and stop ruining everyone's fun by knocking passes down.

—*THE ONION*

• • •

He is the best player I've scouted in twenty-five years. He is the top prospect I've graded in twenty years.
—INDIANAPOLIS COLTS OWNER JIM IRSAY ON QB ANDREW LUCK

• • •

Adrian and I talked [after his knee injury], and I told him that he'll be the guy that people will look at and say, "Wow, look at Adrian Peterson. He's just as good or better than he was before the surgery."
—MINNESOTA VIKINGS COACH LESLIE FRAZIER, AFTER ADRIAN PETERSON TORE HIS ACL IN 2011. HE RETURNED THE FOLLOWING YEAR AND FELL NINE YARDS SHORT OF SETTING THE ALL-TIME RUSHING RECORD FOR A SEASON

• • •

Andrew Luck

You know, it's the moment when reality hits you—you have to trust your own eyes and make a split-second decision in terms of how you're going to get that young man [Adrian Peterson] on the ground. I'm glad I'm not a defensive coordinator to have to answer that one.
—Minnesota Vikings running backs coach
James Saxon

• • •

You really can't put it into words. The things he does on and off the field speak for themselves.
—New Orleans Saints receiver Marques Colston on
QB Drew Brees

• • •

I just felt that energy in New Orleans. From the very beginning there was a genuine feeling that they wanted me there. They believe I can come back from this shoulder injury and lead them to a championship. They were as confident as I am, and that meant a lot.
—Drew Brees

• • •

Troy [Polamalu] could be voted our M.V.P. every year.
—Pittsburgh Steelers linebacker James Harrison,
in 2009

• • •

We just have to play better when I'm not in there or play
easier teams.
—Former Chicago Bears linebacker Brian Urlacher

• • •

I am not better than anyone else just because I play football.
—NFL QB Tim Tebow

• • •

We have a great deal of respect for Tim Tebow.
Unfortunately, things did not work out the way we all had
hoped. . . . We wish him the best moving forward.
—Rex Ryan

PART THREE

• • •

COACHES, OWNERS, FANS, AND BROADCASTERS

Those who select football coaching must understand that the justification for football lies in its physical and spiritual values and that the game belongs, essentially, to the players.
—From the *American Football Coaches Association Code of Ethics*

• • •

I'm awfully proud of you guys, really. You've done a hell of a job. But sometimes you just disgust me.
—Vince Lombardi

• • •

Sometimes [Vince Lombardi] seems to hate everybody without regard to race, religion, or national origin.
—Jerry Kramer, from *Instant Replay*

• • •

While jogging off the field and going past the Giants bench, I see this guy who is ranting and raving at [their] defensive players. Then I recognized [Vince Lombardi]. To show you his aggressiveness and intensity, he was yelling at the defensive players and he was the offensive line coach.
—Packers QB Bart Starr, on the first time he saw Vince Lombardi

• • •

I had watched Lombardi at a practice in 1955 when he was still a Giants assistant. I couldn't believe that one man could yell and scream and spout such profanity.
—Kansas City Chiefs coach Hank Stram

• • •

Vince Lombardi

[Vince Lombardi] was the greatest psychologist.
—DAVID MARANISS, FROM *WHEN PRIDE STILL MATTERED*

• • •

Joe Schmidt of the Detroit Lions: "A football player has certain responsibilities. . . . I haven't missed, or been late for, a practice in thirteen years . . . "
Joe Don Looney of the Detroit Lions: "Man, you need a break. You'd better take an afternoon off. Take my word for it."
—FROM *PAPER LION* BY GEORGE PLIMPTON

• • •

A good coach needs three things: a patient wife, a loyal dog, and a great quarterback—not necessarily in that order.
—FORMER MINNESOTA VIKINGS COACH BUD GRANT

• • •

Nobody did it better or longer than the only coach [Don Shula]
to lead his team to the Super Bowl in three decades.
—DON BANKS

• • •

He can take his'n and beat your'n, or he can take your'n and
beat his'n.
—HOUSTON OILERS COACH BUM PHILLIPS ON DON SHULA

• • •

If you think about it, I've never held a job in my life. I went from
being an NFL player to a coach to a broadcaster. I haven't worked
a day in my life.
—JOHN MADDEN

• • •

Well, no . . . but I've only played for him for nine years.
—DALLAS COWBOYS RUNNING BACK WALT GARRISON, WHEN
ASKED IF HE'D EVER SEEN COACH TOM LANDRY SMILE

• • •

Tom Landry's unemotional, analytical approach to life was hard
to grasp until you got used to it.
—DALLAS COWBOYS CORNERBACK CHARLIE WATERS

• • •

Amazing how much stuff you accumulate for that many years.
You wonder why you never cleaned out your files before.
—TOM LANDRY, ON CLEANING OUT HIS OFFICE FOLLOWING HIS
FIRING BY THE DALLAS COWBOYS AFTER TWENTY-NINE YEARS

• • •

Bill Parcells is the only coach in N.F.L. history to take four different teams to the playoffs, but that only begins to set him apart.
—MICHAEL LEWIS

• • •

I got that [baseball bat] because I got a couple of St. Bernards on this team. You know why they're called St. Bernards? Because I got to hit them with a stick to get 'em to do anything.
—BILL PARCELLS

• • •

I was really excited about Parcells. I got a Super Bowl coach. I got one of the best in the business. But, of course my image of him and what was reality, that was a lot different.
—NEW ENGLAND PATRIOTS OWNER ROBERT KRAFT

• • •

They want you to cook the dinner, at least they ought to let you shop for some of the groceries.
—Bill Parcells, on being overridden on personnel decisions in the 1996 draft, after resigning as coach of the Patriots

• • •

Bill is about Bill, and that's the way he is.
—Drew Bledsoe, after Bill Parcells left the New England Patriots to Coach the New York Jets

• • •

The truly great people in this profession are great for years and years. Let's see how I am in ten years.
—Joe Gibbs

• • •

Nobody in football should be called a genius. A genius is a guy like Norman Einstein.
—JOE THEISMANN

• • •

Running a football franchise is not unlike running any other business: You start first with a structural format and then find the people who can implement it.
—BILL WALSH

• • •

The pressure I felt in coaching was not put on me by [the team owners]. It was put on me by me, myself, my own pride.
—DICK VERMEIL

• • •

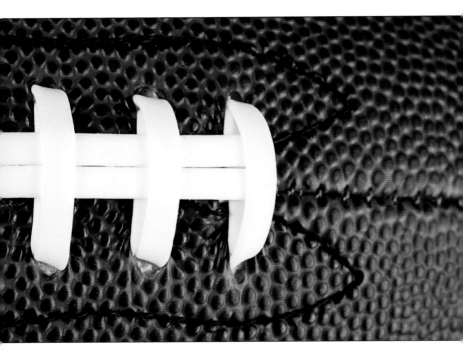

What are you as a coach? You're a glorified teacher. That's all you are.
—NEW YORK GIANTS ASSISTANT COACH KEVIN GILBRIDE

• • •

Doesn't every adult male in America want to own his own football team?
RANKIN MACEACHERN SMITH, THE ORIGINAL OWNER OF THE ATLANTA FALCONS

• • •

[Dallas Cowboys owner Jerry Jones] looked, I imagined, like a collector for a loan shark. I was certain he had the tact and sensitive heart of a hit man. I even created a crime for him—moral assault and battery on Tom Landry.
—GALYN WILKINS, *FORT-WORTH STAR TELEGRAM*

• • •

The first time you meet Al [Davis] he might strike you as a wise guy from Brooklyn. First looks can be deceiving. He has a leer and a knowing smile, but he certainly isn't a popoff and is anything but a wise guy. He's an educated, intelligent, dedicated coach and executive.

—Jack Gallagher, *Houston Post*

• • •

I don't care what others think, so long as I satisfy myself.

—Al Davis

• • •

People think that if you were a Rooney you could automatically work for the Steelers. That wasn't true. You had to really show some genuine interest and dedication. . . . My mom got me a job selling tickets. Hey, it was a start.

—Art Rooney Jr.

• • •

Look at all the talent [Art Rooney Jr.] helped develop. His '74
draft is the greatest in NFL history.
—PAUL ZIMMERMAN

• • •

You're not getting Prince Charming. But give [Bill Belichick]
some leeway and he'll deliver for you.
—CLEVELAND BROWNS OWNER ART MODELL TO NEW
ENGLAND PATRIOTS OWNER ROBERT KRAFT

• • •

Bill Belichick is a good guy and a great coach . . . but he becomes
suspicious if you ask him to give his full name. He figures that no
matter what he says, he could be giving away information that
could aid the opposition. He'll talk for twenty minutes, but when
you look at your notes, where's the meat?
—DICK ENBERG

• • •

You're going to get fired in this business. You're going to quit. You're going to get fired and run out of more jobs than you can count. . . . Sometimes it's in your control, but most of the time it's not. If you're going to have a family, make sure you have some-place that your family can always call home. They need that one stable place, a place that they know they can come back to every year and it will be there forever.

—BILL BELICHICK

• • •

Probably the dumbest firing in history. Do they have any idea how hard it is to win 14 games in this league? Are you kidding me? You fire a guy like Marty Shottenheimer? They [the San Diego Chargers] probably just cursed themselves forever.

—AN NFL GM

• • •

John Harbaugh

Steve [Bisciotti] made it very clear he had made his decision and this was what he was going to do. Here's your $18 million now go away.
—Brian Billick, on his firing by the Baltimore Ravens with three years left on his contract

• • •

Leisure time should be between 2 AM and 5:30 AM when you are sleeping. That way you can combine, into one time frame, two healthy methods to rejuvenate.
—George Allen

• • •

My wife one time got on me when I came home early. It was eleven at night.
—Rex Ryan

• • •

The jaw juts out, the eyes widen, and the mouth turns downward
into a bitter arch.
—DEJAN KOVACEVIC, ON BILL COWHER

• • •

To this day, the most fun I had was at [The University of] Miami.
That's not to take anything away from the Cowboys, but pro
coaching is really more of a grind.
—JIMMY JOHNSON

• • •

Jimmy [Johnson] didn't know any of the damn plays, but you
could break your arm and that dude would make you believe it
didn't hurt.
—DALLAS COWBOYS OFFENSIVE LINEMAN KEVIN GOGAN

• • •

I know I can't cut you [to player #1]. But you [player #2] better play your ass off this weekend, because you might be gone by Monday.
—JIMMY JOHNSON

• • •

It's pretty funny to think of Coach [Tom] Coughlin and Flava Flav hugging it out.
—ELI MANNING

• • •

We saw this naked woman, running hard. But she didn't realize how long a football field is. Around midfield she started running out of gas, like a lineman running back a fumble. She slowed down and staggered away. But she got a nice round of applause.
—TOM FLORES, THEN AN ASSISTANT COACH WITH THE OAKLAND RAIDERS

• • •

Say that your child went to prison but you would not want to embarrass him because of that embarrassment and failure. The [Cleveland] Browns have been in prison for most of the past 10 years. I have not given up on them and still visit them every fall on the shores of Lake Erie
—Lindsay Dudas, Cleveland Browns fan

• • •

Sharks are as tough as those football fans who take their shirts off during games in Chicago in January, only more intelligent.
—Dave Barry

• • •

You go around the city and people point you out. I thought the city and the fans were great. I never met a bad fan there. Philadelphia is a great sports town.
—Former Eagle Dennis Harrison

• • •

Those famously churlish Philadelphia [Eagles] fans cannot hide behind the urban legends. The truth is out there: they simply booed Santa Claus.
—*ASSOCIATED PRESS*

• • •

When I hit the end zone, and the snowballs started, I was waving my finger at the crowd, saying 'You're not getting anything for Christmas.'
—FRANK OLIVIO, WHO DRESSED AS SANTA CLAUS

• • •

Don't drink too much. Don't hit anybody. You'll be fine.
—ROBERT DE NIRO AS PAT SOLITANO TO HIS SON (BRADLEY COOPER) PAT SOLITANO JR., BEFORE AN EAGLES TAILGATE PARTY IN *SILVER LININGS PLAYBOOK*

• • •

They don't play in between the lines. I do. You know what?
Guys who yell that stuff aren't fans; they're jerks. I can't let them
bother me.
—RAY LEWIS

• • •

It was an ideal day for football—too cold for the spectators and
too cold for the players.
—RED SMITH

• • •

While the Detroit Lions are one of a handful of teams that have
never even played in a Super Bowl, these days you are not looked
upon as a lunatic if you say out loud that day is not too far away.
—PAULA PASCHE, FROM *100 THINGS LIONS FANS SHOULD
KNOW AND DO BEFORE THEY DIE*

• • •

Pittsburgh is a throwback town. You see people walking around in Jack Lambert and Jack Ham jerseys. And that was 30 years ago.
—A Steelers fan

• • •

I grew up on play-by-plays and *Monday Night Football* at a time when the Vikings were the Purple People Eaters and the team practiced in a park that doubled as a livestock showing ground.
—Minnesota Senator Amy Klobuchar

• • •

I'm pretty serious about my fantasy football.
—*New York Times* statistician Nate Silver

• • •

My favorite water cooler topic is fantasy football. I used to make fun of friends for doing it and now I'm obsessed.
—John Krasinski

• • •

Fantasy football is not only a good thing, but a great thing.
—Jay Mohr

• • •

Most Sundays, with the exception of football Sundays, I work,
because I don't take days off . . .
—Robert Caro, biographer

• • •

[In the fall of 1960], ours was a small football-watching community which simply evolved of itself, a few of us gathering faithfully
each Sunday afternoon at a local bar to watch the games. . . . We
were, I recognize now, a beer commercial before there were beer
commercials about people like us.
—David Halberstam

• • •

We love the Titans. And we're Packers fans also because Brett Favre is one of our best friends. But we live in Tennessee so we're Titans fans.
—TIM MCGRAW

• • •

It allows me to have time with my husband during football season. If I did not enjoy football, it would almost be like living alone.
—FAITH HILL

• • •

If your man is a sports enthusiast, you may have to resign yourself to his spouting off in a monotone on a prize fight, football game or pennant race.
—MARILYN MONROE

• • •

Larry Fitzgerald

The football season is like pain. You forget how terrible it is until
it seizes you again.
—SALLY QUINN

• • •

I'm not necessarily intimidated by really jocky guys. I can talk
football with them, you know what I mean?
—JOAN JETT

• • •

If there's going to be a lot of questions about football, then this is
going to be the shortest press conference in history . . . because I
don't know anything.
—BRUCE SPRINGSTEEN

• • •

People don't seem to get the connection with being a Christian
and being a Raiders fan. Seems to be contrary to them.
But taking castoffs and bringing them to glory is very harmonic
to the scriptures and the teachings of Christ. I kind of dig
the paradox.
—MARK SHELTON, PROFESSIONAL WRESTLER AND
CORRECTIONS OFFICER

• • •

I'll never forget my first Monday-night game. I had a ton of tackles and Howard [Cosell] loved me . "Phil Vil-a-pi-anno from Bowling Green State University!" The way he said your name made you special. That's when I really saw the power of the *Monday Night* game.
—PHIL VILLAPIANO, LINEBACKER FOR THE OAKLAND RAIDERS AND BUFFALO BILLS

• • •

I'm going to be the most famous name in all of broadcasting.
—HOWARD COSELL

• • •

Al Michaels is a good announcer. I think Keith Jackson is a terrific announcer. I always loved him on *Monday Night Football.* I never understood why they got rid of him.
—JOHN TURTURRO

• • •

Howard Cosell to Frank Gifford and Don Meredith: "Gentlemen, your respective teams are performing a comedy of errors." Don Meredith to Cosell: "Well, Howard, at least we have respective teams."
—*ABC Monday Night Football* game between the Giants and Cowboys

• • •

Clearly, the problem with *Monday Night Football* is that most of the games are between boring teams no one cares very much about, not whether the nation needs more or less of Dennis Miller as a commentator (I would vote for less).
—David Halberstam, from "How I Fell in Love with the NFL"

• • •

Monday Night is a stage where everybody watches. It's more than a game, it's an event.
—Joe Theismann

• • •

PART FOUR

THE RIVALRIES

Football is the only team sport in America that conjures up visions of Roman gladiators . . . sometimes with a Civil War feel, like when the Jets play the Giants in New York or the Dallas Cowboys play the Washington Redskins
—HOWIE LONG

• • •

What the Monsters of the Midway figure to do to the New Yorkers [Giants] is enough to make women weep and strong men shudder.
—ARTHUR DALY, *NEW YORK TIMES*, BEFORE THE 1941 NFL CHAMPIONSHIP GAME

• • •

Titans are bigger and stronger than Giants.
—HARRY WISMER, OWNER OF THE NEW YORK TITANS OF THE AFL, THE TEAM THAT BECAME THE JETS

• • •

I drilled his ass. I hit him and drove his ass to the ground.
—Oakland Raiders safety George Atkinson on
hitting Steelers wide receiver Lynn Swann

• • •

We hated them and they hated us. There was respect, too, but
that week we pretty much stuck to hate.
—Steelers linebacker Andy Russell, on the
Pittsburgh-Oakland rivalry

• • •

This might be the first game where a penalty flag is thrown in the
parking lot.
—An NFL executive before a Steelers-Raiders
playoff game in 1976

• • •

Jack Lambert is the defender of all that is right [after Lambert leveled Cowboys safety Cliff Harris for what he considered a cheap shot].
—Pittsburgh Steelers coach Chuck Noll

• • •

The rulebook doesn't cover the hand of God.
—Chuck Noll, when asked if Franco Harris's Immaculate reception against the Raiders was Legal

• • •

Every game was a terrifying adventure, win or lose, and the Raiders of the 70s usually won—except in Pittsburgh, where cruel things happened and many dreams died horribly.
—Hunter S. Thompson

• • •

One more play [against the Steelers] was all we needed. How
come time always runs out on us?
—RAIDERS QB KEN STABLER

• • •

[The Steelers of the early 70s were] probably the greatest collection of football talent ever assembled, a team with absolutely
no weaknesses.
—FORMER NY GIANTS GM GEORGE YOUNG

• • •

Dear John and Chuck: A review of your September 12 [1976]
game indicates that your "intense rivalry" of recent years could
be on the verge of erupting into something approaching
pure violence.
—NFL COMMISSIONER PETE ROZELLE, IN A LETTER TO JOHN
MADDEN AND CHUCK NOLL

• • •

We're in the huddle and the play comes in from the sideline to run the ball. We're up by 50 points, but [Mike] Phipps hadn't had a lot of opportunity to play. They're telling him to run the ball and he goes, "I don't think so." So he starts putting it back up in the air. It was a beautiful thing. Were we trying to rub it in? Absolutely. We wanted 70 points.
—CHICAGO BEARS OFFENSIVE LINEMAN DAN JIGGETS ON A 1980 GAME AGAINST THE PACKERS, WHICH THE BEARS WON 61-7

• • •

We don't need luck, we just need to be in position. [Chicago QB] Jay Cutler will throw us the ball.
—GREEN BAY DEFENSIVE BACK CHARLES WOODSON

• • •

When I arrived at the box suites, I was taken to a box next to the one occupied by [George] Halas and his son. . . . I found out why they weren't sitting with me as soon as the game started. They began screaming all sorts of obscenities . . . at the officials and opposing players and never stopped.
—BOB HOPE, ON ATTENDING A BEARS-PACKERS GAME IN THE 70S

• • •

Brett Favre and John Elway before Super Bowl XXXII

That's kind of what everyone was hoping for—those two teams.
The only thing better would have been if it were here at Lambeau.
—A Green Bay Packers fan, before the January 2011
NFC championship game between the Packers and
Chicago Bears

• • •

The Vikings play football like a guy laying carpet. The Raiders
play like a guy jumping through a skylight with a machine gun.
—Jim Murray, Los Angeles Times,
before Super Bowl XI

• • •

The Chiefs-Raiders rivalry was about as spirited as any in professional football in my time. They didn't like us and we didn't
like them.
—Jim Lynch, former Chiefs linebacker

• • •

Every year [in the sixties and seventies] to even think about a
Super Bowl, you knew you had to go through the Raiders or you
had to go through the Kansas City Chiefs.
—FORMER OAKLAND RAIDERS CORNERBACK WILLIE BROWN

• • •

The old guys got tired of reading that that they were old guys. We
just reached down and came up with some gut football.
—MINNESOTA VIKINGS CENTER MICK TINGELHOFF, ON
THE VIKINGS NFC CHAMPIONSHIP VICTORY AGAINST THE
DALLAS COWBOYS IN 1973

• • •

After the game, the press asked me about the play. I said I closed
my eyes and said a Hail Mary. The next day some writer dubbed
it the Hail Mary pass.
—ROGER STAUBACH, DALLAS COWBOYS QB, ON HIS
NFC CHAMPIONSHIP GAME-WINNING PASS AGAINST THE
MINNESOTA VIKINGS IN 1975

• • •

It was just one play, but it changed the fortunes of an organization, and it changed people's lives.
—New York Giants QB Joe Pisarcik, after his fumble with 31 seconds remaining against the Philadelphia Eagles was returned for a game-losing touchdown

• • •

I'm just sitting back there thinking, "They're really not going to kick it to me."
—Philadelphia Eagles DeSean Jackson, whose 65-yard punt return for a winning touchdown against the Giants erased a 21-point lead

• • •

I've never been around anything like this in my life. It's about as empty as you get to feel in this business.
—New York Giants coach Tom Coughlin, after Jackson's punt return

• • •

You don't have to play bombs away. Your defense has to give the ball back to you every time, and you have to be protected well.
—Buffalo Bills QB Frank Reich, after he led the Bills to a 32-point comeback win over the Miami Dolphins in the 1992 AFC Wild Card Game

• • •

How am I going to play with a splint? Hell, you can't play with a splint on your throwing hand. And of all places in Minnesota.
—Green Bay quarterback Brett Favre, after leading the Packers to a 30-27 win against the Vikings

• • •

I have to admit, being in Lambeau [Field] was a pretty neat experience. . . . It was, like, 15 degrees and there were people out tailgating and having a ball. . . . These folks had this stuff down to a science; I was impressed. I had never seen so many grills fired up at one time, not to mention the sheer volume of beer that was being consumed. . . . And it was a noon kickoff!
—Ross Bernstein, Minnesota Vikings fan, from *I Love/ Hate Brett Favre*

• • •

Needless to say, I wasn't exactly expecting the stadium to give me a standing ovation when we took the field in Miami. Given our past, I wanted to play so hard and so tough that we'd absolutely kill them.
—NEW YORK JETS COACH REX RYAN

• • •

I want them to know, and they know, that I think we're going to beat them. It doesn't really matter who says what, but we're going to be ourselves. And we're coming up there to take our swing. We'll see if we land that punch to win the game.
—NEW YORK JETS COACH REX RYAN, ON THE NEW ENGLAND PATRIOTS

• • •

I never came here to kiss Bill Belichick's, you know, rings.
—REX RYAN

• • •

I've known the 49ers for years and I've just grown to hate them.
—CAROLINA PANTHERS LINEBACKER KEVIN GREENE

• • •

I think it's shameful. There's no place for anything like that in our game. It's too great a game. I think certain times players cross the line, and you've got to take care of business.
—SEATTLE SEAHAWKS COACH MIKE HOLMGREN, AFTER THE 49ERS TERRELL OWENS AUTOGRAPHED THE BALL AFTER SCORING A TOUCHDOWN

• • •

Oh, how the mighty have fallen
Irvin and Smith left Redskins sprawlin'
Roused from the undefeated dream
By that oh-so-hated Dallas team!

. . .

It's a tough loss but don't be sore
Wait 'til the playoffs when we will beat you once more.
—CONGRESSMAN DICK ARMEY (R-TEXAS 26TH DISTRICT) IN
AN ADDRESS DELIVERED ON THE HOUSE FLOOR

• • •

I Root for Two Teams: The Redskins and Anyone Playing Dallas
—SLOGAN ON T-SHIRTS SOLD IN THE WASHINGTON AREA

• • •

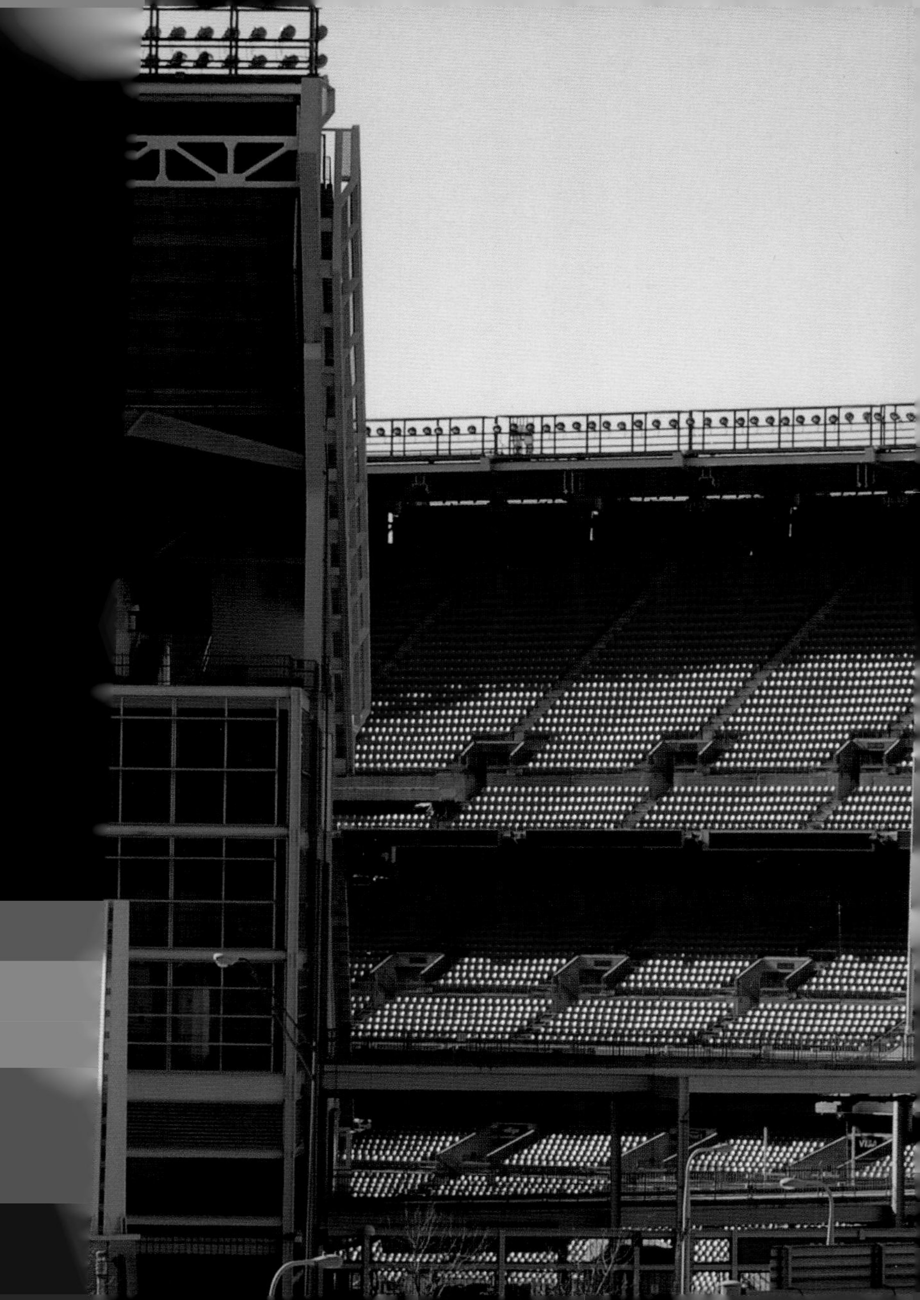

[The Dallas Cowboys is] one of the two most efficient organizations of the 20th century. . . . The Third Reich [is number one].
—BEANO COOK

• • •

They threw the book at us. Sometimes we did good with it and sometimes we didn't. If a veteran quarterback's in there, maybe it's different. But they did it to Manning, and they did it to a rookie.
—STEELERS QB BEN ROETHLISBERGER, AFTER LOSING TO THE NEW ENGLAND PATRIOTS DURING HIS ROOKIE SEASON

• • •

The Giants shouldn't take their eyes off their ultimate goal: looking like garbage for half the season then embarrassing the Patriots.
—*THE ONION*, "KEYS TO THE MATCHUPS," 9/20/2012

• • •

I hate losing to them. I hate losing to anybody, but to them it's a lot worse
—PITTSBURGH STEELERS LINEBACKER JAMES HARRISON ON THE BALTIMORE RAVENS

• • •

Drew Brees and his family after Super Bowl XLIV

PART FIVE

THE CHAMPIONSHIPS

I remember Frank Gifford putting them ahead early in the fourth quarter, but we came back to tie it with about two minutes left in the game. Johnny Unitas drove us down the field with just a few seconds to go, and we were able to tie it. . . . Once the game ended, we all just stood there, expecting it to be a tie, and then the officials said that they were going to flip a coin. . . . Alan Ameche [later] scored on a one-yard touchdown. It was unbelievable.

—Raymond Berry, Baltimore Colts wide receiver, on the 1958 championship game with the New York Giants

• • •

When you know what you're doing, you're not intercepted. The Giants were jammed up at the line and not expecting a pass. If [my receiver] had been covered, I would have thrown it out of bounds. It's just that I'd rather win a game like this by a touchdown than by a field goal.

—Johnny Unitas after the 1958 NFL championship game

• • •

You know, everyone has called it the greatest game ever played. Oh, that overtime period and the TV exposure might have given it a little more importance, but I played the game just like any other.
—Johnny Unitas

• • •

No excuses. The Bears won it and I can't take that away from them. It just hurts a little bit when you see those films.
—Allie Sherman, coach of the New York Giants, after his team lost to the Chicago Bears in the 1963 NFL championship game, 14-10

• • •

That may have been the biggest block I ever made in my life.
—Jerry Kramer, on his block of the Cowboys' Jethro Pugh that allowed Bart Starr to score in the 1967 NFL title game

• • •

I believe we should "coin a phrase" for the championship game. . . .
I have kiddingly called it the Super Bowl, which obviously can be
improved upon.
—Kansas City Chiefs owner Lamar Hunt, in a letter
to Pete Rozelle

• • •

Will the Super Bowl attract a super crowd? . . . Although no
ticket scale has been affixed yet . . . [the general manager of the
Los Angeles Coliseum] has heard rumblings of a $12 top.
—The *New York Times*, December 8, 1966

• • •

John Elway tackled by the New York Giants during Super Bowl XXI

Dallas is a better team. Kansas City is a good team, but they don't even rate with some of the teams in our division. There. That's what you wanted me to say, isn't it?
—Vince Lombardi, after his Green Bay Packers defeated the Kansas City Chiefs in Super Bowl I

• • •

If we don't win this game, I'll walk home to Detroit.
—The Lions' Alex Karras, as he refused to shake the hand of the Denver Broncos captain before an NFL/AFL exhibition game in 1967, which the Broncos won 13-7

• • •

We're a better team than Baltimore.
—New York Jets QB Joe Namath, prior to Super Bowl III

• • •

I remember walking out . . . and seeing Johnny Unitas there. I thought about when I was in high school and guys called me "Joey U" and now I'm out on the field with him.
—JOE NAMATH, RECALLING THE COIN TOSS PRIOR TO SUPER BOWL III

• • •

I want all of you to remember how we feel right now, and I don't ever want to feel this way again.
—DON SHULA TO HIS BALTIMORE COLTS, AFTER THEY LOST SUPER BOWL VI TO THE DALLAS COWBOYS

• • •

Probably Duane Thomas's attitude toward the media during Super Bowl week got me the MVP. Duane was the guy Miami couldn't stop . . . but they probably said, "Roger did okay, let's give it to him."
—ROGER STAUBACH

• • •

We dominated the league in the 1970s. We did as much as Pittsburgh, the 49ers, or the Miami Dolphins of that era. But I didn't realize then, as I do now, how important it is to win the Super Bowl. We did well, but we never won that last one, so we will never be associated with those great teams of the past.
—Former Minnesota Vikings QB Fran Tarkenton

• • •

You should try a down-and-in pattern to [Paul] Warfield. I think it would work.
—President Richard Nixon to Miami Coach Don Shula before Super Bowl VI

• • •

Some football genius Nixon is.
—Dallas safety Cliff Harris, after the Pass play to
Warfield failed and the Cowboys beat the Dolphins

• • •

Minor adjustments to the place kicker's measurements may be
needed to ensure that the kicking foot makes the proper contact
with the ball.
—Steve Libassi, from *Placekicking Fundamentals
and Techniques*

• • •

I hit the ball with my hands. It went up . . . and Mike Bass of the Redskins caught it and went down the sideline 49 yards for a touchdown. All of a sudden the score was 14-7 with three and a half minutes to play.
—GARO YEPREMIEN, MIAMI DOLPHINS KICKER, AFTER SUPER BOWL VII

• • •

Garo, I forgive you. But if we [had] lost, I would have killed you.
—DOLPHINS COACH DON SHULA

• • •

When it was all over, Lynn Swann and the Steelers had won 21-17 and repeated as the champions of professional madness.
—DAN JENKINS, SPORTS ILLUSTRATED, ON SUPER BOWL X

• • •

Today I relaxed, felt good and had fun. I just tried to go out there and help win a football game.
—Terry Bradshaw, Super Bowl XIII MVP

• • •

Halfway through the decade, we realized that we had a great team and that we could do great things.
—Franco Harris, whose Pittsburgh Steelers won four championships in the 1970s—in 1974, 1975, 1978, and 1979

• • •

I looked down the field and I saw that patch of grass between our huddle and their goal posts, and I thought "That's it. That one patch of grass between us and the Super Bowl."
—San Francisco 49ers center Fred Quillan, on the 1981 NFL championship game

• • •

Terry Bradshaw hands off to Franco Harris during Super Bowl XIII

Sometimes time runs out.
—DALLAS COWBOYS COACH TOM LANDRY, AFTER HIS TEAM
LOST TO THE 49ERS IN THE 1981 NFC CHAMPIONSHIP GAME

• • •

I was on a team that took on the world. It wasn't just winning the
Super Bowl. Hell, we got a gold record. We got a platinum video.
We talked about it and we did it.
—RICHARD DENT, ON HIS 1985 CHICAGO BEARS

• • •

We should've won (more than) one, but the one we won is bigger
and better than anybody ever won.
—RICHARD DENT

• • •

Dynasties are the ones that win two, three, four Super Bowls, like the Steelers and the Cowboys did. The one knock on us was we won one.
—MIKE DITKA, COACH OF THE 1985 CHICAGO BEARS

● ● ●

We buried all the ghosts today. They're all gone.
—BILL PARCELLS, AFTER HIS NEW YORK GIANTS DEFEATED DENVER TO WIN SUPER BOWL XXI

● ● ●

Think about what would happen if we played Buffalo on the practice field: We'd kick the hell out of them. It would be no contest. When you're preparing for this game, focus on the fact that nobody will be watching.
—DALLAS COACH JIMMY JOHNSON, BEFORE THE COWBOYS DRUBBED THE BILLS 52-17 IN SUPER BOWL XXVII

● ● ●

We both start crying, and Coach is comparing this moment to Joe Louis knocking out Max Schmeling. Then he told me that I would never, ever, understand the impact of what I just had accomplished until I got older, and he was right.
—FORMER REDSKINS QB DOUG WILLIAMS, ON BEING THE FIRST BLACK QB TO WIN A SUPER BOWL

• • •

Winning is better than anything. Better than sex. Better than Christmas morning.
—BILL PARCELLS, AFTER HIS NEW YORK GIANTS WON THEIR SECOND SUPER BOWL

• • •

You don't get used to losing. You don't just accept it. This loss hurts as badly as any of the others. We would go through that period of mourning. We would own up. We would recognize the good. We would make a plan.
—MARV LEVY, WHOSE BUFFALO BILLS LOST FOUR CONSECUTIVE SUPER BOWLS

• • •

I remember going back on the field after one of our Super Bowls. The stadium was empty, the field was deserted, and Charles Mann, our great defensive end, said, "You know, Coach, getting here was the fun."
—Former Washington Redskins coach Joe Gibbs

• • •

If I had a full migraine, there's probably no way I finish that game.
—Super Bowl XXXII MVP Terrell Davis, whose Denver Broncos defeated the Green Bay Packers in 1998

• • •

Probably the greatest feeling of relief I've had in my life was when I saw T.D. come out of the locker room with his helmet on for the second half. All I was looking for was T.D. coming out, period.
—Denver Broncos owner Pat Bowlen

• • •

From that moment on, every great defensive play in Super Bowl will always be measured by Mike's. And I doubt if they'll ever be a greater play made on the final play of a Super Bowl with one second left on the clock. It just isn't possible.
—St. Louis Rams coach Dick Vermeil after linebacker Mike Jones prevented Tennessee Titan Kevin Dyson from scoring the winning touchdown as time expired in Super Bowl XXXIV

• • •

Didn't make it. Didn't make it. No. No. That's it. We win. That's the game. It's over. We're world champions.
—Dick Vermeil, as the final play unfolded during Super Bowl XXXIV

• • •

You may not win the Super Bowl. Your kids may not go on to be doctors and lawyers and everything may not go perfectly. That doesn't mean it was a bad plan or the wrong thing. It's just like a football season. Everything's not going to go perfect.
—TONY DUNGY

• • •

For Mike [Shanahan, the Denver Broncos coach, Super Bowl XXXIII] was personal. I've never seen him more ready for a football game. I knew it meant more to him than any game he has ever coached.
—JOHN ELWAY, AFTER THE BRONCOS DEFEATED DAN REEVES'S ATLANTA FALCONS 34-19

• • •

You give us 7 and we might win. If our offense comes out and plays well, we've got a very good chance to win.
—Ray Lewis, before his Baltimore Ravens defeated the New York Giants 34-7 in Super Bowl XXXV

• • •

Our main goal was to have the first shutout in Super Bowl history. Unfortunately, we gave up a kickoff return.
—Baltimore Ravens safety Ron Woodson

• • •

I honestly believe this team [the 2005 Philadelphia Eagles] will win the NFC championship once we get there. There's no doubt in my mind. I feel like I've done what I had to do. I set the table. Now all they have to do is go eat.
—Terrell Owens, who was sidelined with a broken leg late in the season

• • •

I'm telling you, this is our game.
—Indianapolis Colts coach Tony Dungy to QB Peyton Manning, before the 2006 AFC Championship against the New England Patriots

• • •

Well, once you get to the point where you have to put six diamonds on a ring, it's pretty hard to be modest about what you're trying to do.
—Art Rooney II, after the Pittsburgh Steelers won Super Bowl XLIII

• • •

[Safety Rodney] Harrison made as good a play as he could have made on it. I don't think there's anything else he could have done.
—Patriots coach Bill Belichick, on the circus catch David Tyree made to keep the Giants alive in Super Bowl XLII, which New York won, 17-14

• • •

Oh my God, I don't believe it. They won us the game. Our offense came through for us when we really needed it. We went out there and gave up a big touchdown, and our offense came through at the end.
—Pittsburgh linebacker James Harrison, on the Steelers 27-23 victory over the Arizona Cardinals in Super Bowl XLIII

• • •

The Saints were very lucky to get it. It wasn't like the Colts were out to lunch. But they had the aggressiveness and the guts to do it. A lot of times, that's all you need.
—Mike Westhoff, special teams coach, on the Saints executing a successful onside kick to start the second half of Super Bowl XLIV

• • •

We had been the tragic Saints from tragic New Orleans, but neither of us was tragic anymore.
—Sean Payton, New Orleans Saints head coach

• • •

New Orleans may not be the swiftest when it comes to amassing Super Bowl victories. But let me tell you: this city knows how to throw a parade.
—SEAN PAYTON

• • •

Being from a small school, I understand how that whole thing goes. I wasn't 6-5, 220 pounds, or I didn't have off-the-wall statistics. But I'd rather be here for the Super Bowl now than [at] the Combine.
—NEW YORK GIANTS WIDE RECEIVER VICTOR CRUZ, ON SUPER BOWL XLVI

• • •

The pass went for 38 yards, a pointed answer to the yearlong question of whether Eli [Manning] was an elite player.
—JUDY BATTISTA, *NEW YORK TIMES*, ON ELI MANNING'S PASS TO MARIO MANNINGHAM WITH UNDER FOUR MINUTES REMAINING IN SUPER BOWL XLVI. THE GIANTS CAME FROM BEHIND TO DEFEAT THE PATRIOTS, 21-17

• • •

The moment doesn't get too big. We are comfortable. We've been there before. We've failed before. We've succeeded before. We are not worried about the outcome. We just go out there and play football, execute and we believe that if we do that, and do that to our ability, then eventually it is going to work out.
—JOE FLACCO, MVP QB OF SUPER BOWL XLVII

• • •

How could it be any other way? It's never pretty. It's never perfect. But it is us.
—BALTIMORE RAVENS COACH JOHN HARBAUGH, AFTER SUPER BOWL XLVII

• • •

It helps to win that championship.
—MARV LEVY, HALL OF FAME COACH OF THE BUFFALO BILLS, ON LOSING FOUR CONSECUTIVE SUPER BOWLS, 1991-1994

• • •

I'd trade every record we broke to be Super Bowl champs.
—Miami Dolphins QB Dan Marino

• • •

Individual commitment to a group effort—that is what makes a team work, a company work, a society work, a civilization work.
—Vince Lombardi

• • •

WORKS AND AUTHORS QUOTED

Books
Michael W. Austin (ed.)
Football and Philosophy: Going Deep (2008)

Bob Berghaus
The First America's Team: The 1962 Green Bay Packers (2011)

Roy Blount Jr.
About Three Bricks Shy of a Load: A Highly Irregular Lowdown on the Year the Steelers Were Super but Missed the Bowl (1974)

Terry Bradshaw, with David Fischer
It's Only a Game (2001)

Tom Callahan
Johnny U.: The Life and Times of Johnny Unitas (2007)

Chuck Carlson
Game of My Life, Green Bay Packers: Memorable Stories of Packers Football (2012)

Dave Christensen and James A. Peterson
Coaching Offensive Linemen (2003)

Kevin Cook
The Last Headbangers: NFL Football in the Rowdy, Reckless '70s (2012)

Myron Cope
The Game that Was: An Illustrated Account of the Tumultuous Early Days of Pro Football (1970)
Double Yoi! (2002)

Roger Craig
Tales from the San Francisco 49ers Sideline (2012)

Tom Danyluk
The Super '70s: Memories from Pro Football's Greatest Era (2012)

Don DeLillo
End Zone (1986)

Jeff Duncan
Tales from the New Orleans Saints Sideline (2012)

Ken Dunnavant
America's Quarterback: Bart Starr and the Rise of the National Football League (2011)

John Eisenberg
That First Season: How Vince Lombardi Took the Worst Team in the NFL Football and Set It on the Path to Glory (2010)

Dick Enberg
Oh My! (2004)

Larry Felser
The Birth of the New NFL: How the 1966 NFL/AFL Merger Transformed Pro Football (2008)

Scott Fowler
Year of the Cat: How the Carolina Panthers Clawed Their Way to the Brink of the Super Bowl (2007)

Mike Freeman
Undefeated: Inside the 1972 Miami Dolphins Perfect Season (2012)

Peter Golenbock
Landry's Boys: An Oral History of a Team and an Era (2005)

Forrest Gregg and Andrew O'Toole
Winning in the Trenches: A Lifetime of Football (2009)

Tony Grossi
Tales from the Cleveland Browns Sideline (2012)

David Halberstam
"How I Fell in Love with the NFL" (2001)
Everything they Had: Sports Writing from David Halberstam (2009)

Phil Hanrahan
Life After Favre: The Green Bay Packers Usher in the Aaron Rodgers Era (2011)

Cliff Harris and Charlie Waters
Tales from the Dallas Cowboys Sideline (2012)

Dan Jenkins
Rude Behavior (2010)

Jerry Kramer and Dick Schaap
Instant Replay (1968)

Mark Kriegel
Namath: A Biography (2004)

Tom Layden,
Blood, Sweat, and Chalk: How the Great Coaches Built Today's Game (2010)

Adam Lazarus
Best of Rivals: Joe Montana, Steve Young and the Inside Story Behind the NFL's Greatest Quarterback Controversy (2012)

Marv Levy
Where Else Would you Rather Be? (2004)

Steve Libassi
Placekicking Fundamentals and Techniques (2005)

Howie Long
Football for Dummies (2011)

David Maraniss,
When Pride Still Mattered (1999)

Michael McCambridge
America's Game: The Epic Story of How Pro Football Captured a Nation (2004)

Bob McGinn and Michael MacCambridge
The Ultimate Super Bowl Book (2012)

Gary Meyers
Coaching Confidential: Inside the Fraternity of NFL Coaches (2012)
The Catch: Two Dynasties, and the Game that Changed the NFL (2010)

Jim Miller and Katy Mayhew
Better to Reign in Hell: Inside the Raiders Fan Empire (2005)

Joe Willie Namath with Richard Schaap
I Can't Wait Until Tomorrow . . . 'Cause I get Better-Looking Every Day (1970)

Michael O'Brien
Vince: A Personal Biography of Vince Lombardi (1987)

Michael Oriard
Reading Football: How the Popular Press Created an American Spectacle (1998)

Sean Payton
Home Team: Coaching the Saints and New Orleans Back to Life (2012)

Ernie Palladino
Lombardi and Landry (2011)

Jeff Pearlman
Boys Will Be Boys: The Glory Days and Party Nights of the Dallas Cowboys Dynasty (2008)

Danny Peary
Super Bowl: The Game of Their Lives—The Definitive Game-by-Game History as Told by the Stars (1997)

Works and Authors Quoted

Terry Pluto
Things I've Learned from Watching the Browns (2010)

Greg Prato
Sack Exchange: The Definitive History of the 1980s New York Jets (2011)

Jerry Rice
Go Long! My Journey Beyond the Game and the Fame (2007)

Jim Saccamano
Game of My Life, Denver Broncos: Memorable Stories of Broncos Football (2012)

Lou Sahadi
Johnny Unitas: America's Quarterback (2004)

Marty Shottenheimer
Martyball: The Life and Triumphs of Marty Shottenheimer, the Coach Who Really Did Win it All (2012)

Sporting News
Complete Super Bowl Book (1995)

Sports Illustrated
Football's Greatest (2009)

Jean-Jacques Taylor
Game of My Life, Dallas Cowboys: Memorable Stories of Cowboys Football (2012)

Hunter S. Thompson
Fear and Loathing on the Campaign Trail '72 (1973)

Ralph Vacchiano
Eli Manning: The Making of a Quarterback (2012)

Bill Walsh, with Glenn Dickey
Building a Champion: On Football and the Making of the 49ers (1992)

Jim Wexell
Tales from Behind the Steel Curtain: The Best Stories of the '79 Steelers (2004)

Matt Winkeljohn
Tales from the Atlanta Falcons Sideline (2012)

Garo Yepremian
Tales from the Miami Dolphins Sideline (2012)

Periodicals
Chicago Tribune
Los Angeles Times
Miami Herald
The New York Times

New York Daily News
New York Post
Oakland Tribune
Philadelphia Daily News
San Francisco Chronicle
The Seattle Times
The Sporting News
Sports Illustrated

Websites
Pro Football Hall of Fame: www.profootballhof.com
ESPN: espn.go.com
espn.go.com/sportscentury/features
The Onion: theonion.com

INDEX

PHOTO CREDITS

Page 74: AP Photo
Page 80: AP Photo/Phil Sandlin
Page 84: AP Photo
Page 88: Thinkstock
Page 95: AP Photo/Nick Waas, File
Page 101: AP Photo/Michael Conroy
Page 104: AP Photo
Page 108: AP Photo/File
Page 112: Thinkstock
Page 116: Thinkstock
Page 121: AP Photo/Evan Vucci
Page 124: Thinkstock
Page 128: Thinkstock
Page 134: AP Photo/Jason Babyak
Page 138: AP Photo/Evan Vucci
Page 145: AP Photo/Dave Martin
Page 148-9: Thinkstock
Page 152: Thinkstock
Page 156-57: Thinkstock
Page 160: AP Photo/Kevin Terrell
Page 165: AP Photo/Reed Saxon
Page 170-1: Thinkstock
Page 174-5: AP Photo
Page 179: Thinkstock
Page 183: Thinkstock